GW00390822

Hereford Cathedral from the River Wye

The Wye Valley and Herefordshire

Passing between the rugged peaks of the Black Mountains on the Welsh border and the more gentle slopes of the Malvern Hills in the east, the Wye Valley is justly renowned as one of the most picturesque areas of Britain. On its 135 mile long journey from its source on the slopes of Plynlimon, deep in the heart of Wales, to the Severn estuary below Chepstow, the River Wye winds through several counties and scenery of rich variety. Wooded gorges, meadows and farmland are interspersed with friendly market towns and villages steeped in history. The area between Ross and Chepstow is especially popular with visitors. Here the river wends its way through the rolling countryside of south Herefordshire and Monmouthshire, where the region is particularly well endowed with ancient castles, a legacy of border unrest in medieval times, historic churches and fine old timbered homesteads. The landscape of the Wye Valley is dramatic yet without extremes; its hills are steep and broad, its meadowland lush, providing grazing for sheep and for the traditional red and white Hereford cattle. This is also the land of the cider apple and the blossom provides a riot of colour in the spring.

The Middle and Lower Baileys, Chepstow Castle

Marten's Tower and Gatehouse, Chepstow Castle

The historic fortress town of **Chepstow** in Gwent is the southern gateway to the Wye Valley. Once a Roman settlement, Chepstow was later to become an important port and ship building centre. The attractive maze of narrow, steep streets contains a number of interesting old buildings, including some fine 17th and 18th century almshouses. The town walls, which are known locally as the Port Walls, originally ran from the castle ditch down to the river. They are well preserved for much of their length and the medieval Town Gate, rebuilt in 1524, houses a small museum in a room over the archway.

West Gate, Chepstow

Chepstow Castle from the River Wye

Strategically positioned on a spur of rock over-looking a bend in the River Wye, **Chepstow Castle** was built to guard the river crossing into Wales. Construction was begun soon after the Norman conquest by William Fitz Osbern and the massive keep dates from this early period. The castle was extended in the 12th and 13th centuries and the outer walls and gatehouse are preserved in excellent condition along with Marten's Tower. This was named after one of the signatories of Charles I's death warrant, Henry Marten, who was imprisoned in the tower for 20 years.

Tintern from Offa's Dyke Path

The delightful village of **Tintern**, with a background of wooded hills sweeping down to the river, is dominated by the ruins of Tintern Abbey. Immortalised by Wordsworth in his poem, 'Lines composed a few miles above Tintern Abbey', this 12th century Cistercian foundation presents one of the most enchanting sights of the whole Wye Valley. Nestling in a loop of the river, the abbey church survives almost intact. With its soaring east end, rose window and fine arches it measures 228 feet long by 150 feet wide across the transepts. Many of the other monastic buildings are also preserved including the chapter house and refectory. Tintern is seen to advantage from 8th century Offa's Dyke. A 168 mile long path, the Offa's Dyke National Trail, meanders along the Welsh border through some of the finest landscape in Britain.

Autumn at Tintern Abbey

Tintern Abbey from the South-east

Tintern Abbey from the South-west

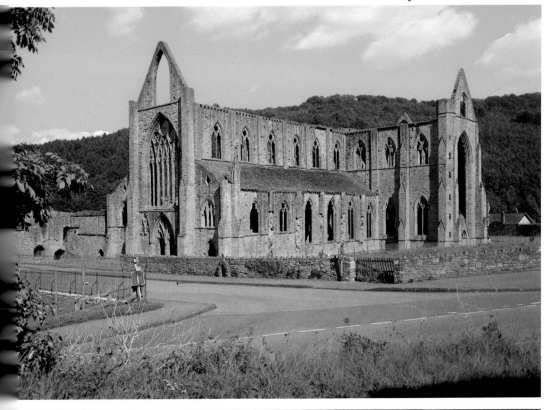

LINES COMPOSED A FEW MILES
ABOVE TINTERN ABBEY

*On Revisiting the Banks
of the Wye during a Tour*

Five years have past; five summers, with the length
  Of five long winters! and again I hear
These waters, rolling from their mountain springs
  With a soft inland murmur – once again
Do I behold these steep and lofty cliffs,
  That on a wild secluded scene impress
Thought of more deep seclusion; and connect
  The Landscape with the quiet of the sky.
...Nor will thou then forget
  That after many wanderings. many years
Of absence, these steep woods and lofty cliffs.
  And this green pastoral landscape, were to me
More dear, both by themselves and for thy sake.

William Wordsworth

Monmouth stands in the centre of three rivers: the Wye, the Trothy and the Monnow. An important centre in Norman times, the castle ruins can still be seen but the most notable feature of the town is the Monnow Bridge. It is the only Norman fortified bridge surviving in Britain and the tower which surmounts it was built in 1260 as one of the four medieval gates into the town. Monmouth also has many fine Tudor and Georgian buildings. At the heart of the town is Agincourt Square, its name a reminder of the town's connection with Henry V. The warrior king was born in the castle and on one side of the square a statue to him stands in a recess in the wall of the splendid 18th century Shire Hall.

Agincourt Square, Monmouth

The Cross, Overmonnow

Separated from Monmouth by the Monnow Gate is the part of the town known as **Overmonnow**, or "the Cappers' Town". It was here that Monmouth caps were made, woollen caps which in Elizabethan times were worn on Sundays and holy days. St. Thomas' Church, Overmonnow became known as the cappers' church.

Wye Bridge, Monmouth

Wye Bridge carries the road which runs from Monmouth along the Wye Valley to Chepstow. Built in 1617 it was widened in the 19th century after the railway attracted more traffic to the town. Facing the bridge are some of the buildings of Monmouth School.

The Monnow Bridge, Monmouth

River Wye from Yat Rock, Symonds Ya

At **Symonds Yat** the calm progress of the river is broken by a series of rapids as it winds through a narrow gorge providing an exhilarating challenge for canoeists. 'Yat' is an old English word meaning gate and originally the yat was a pass through Iron Age fortifications high up on the crag. The hill on the western side of the river, opposite Yat Rock, is called the Great Doward. Below it is the village of Symonds Yat with its two riverside inns, "The Olde Ferrie Inn" and "The Saracens Head". Downstream there are limestone outcrops known as the Seven Sisters Rocks and close by is King Arthur's Cave, through which the river once flowed. Near Whitchurch, at the entrance to Symonds Yat, is the Wye Valley Visitor Centre which gives a fascinating insight into the area.

The River Wye at Symonds Yat

The Great Doward, Symonds Yat

A little upstream from Monmouth the Wye performs a huge four mile loop, at the southern end of which the two stretches of river are only some six hundred yards apart. Sandwiched in the middle is the famous **Yat Rock**. Rising almost sheer from the riverbank to a height of some five hundred feet, this wooded outcrop offers magnificent views from the summit. The majestic prospect northwards across the rolling Herefordshire countryside is the best known in the Wye Valley, and is particularly beautiful when autumn tints colour the woodland.

The Log Cabin, Symonds Yat

The River Wye from Yat Rock, Symonds Yat

Old Ferrie Inn, Symonds Yat

In the south western corner of Gloucestershire, cut off from the rest of the county by the Severn estuary, is the **Forest of Dean.** This ancient woodland provided many of the oak trees from which the wooden warships of England were built and today it is still heavily forested, mainly with oak and beech. It is a peaceful place with nature trails and walks which enable visitors to enjoy the scenery and wildlife. One of the traditional local rights is free mining and in the centre of the forest stands the Speech House, built in 1680 for the control of this and other forest matters. Here the Verderers' Court still meets to conduct its business.

Dean Heritage Centre, Forest of Dean

Speech House, Forest of Dean

Wilton Bridge, Ross-on-Wye

The road from Ross to Goodrich crosses the Wye at **Wilton Bridge** which was built in 1599 to replace an earlier ford. It incorporates some intricate, indented stonework and a quaint four-square stone sundial surmounts a pillar on the bridge. The arch nearest to Wilton was reconstructed after it was damaged during the Civil War. **Goodrich Castle** is impressively situated on a sandstone outcrop overlooking the river. Impregnable on two sides due to the cliffs rising from the river bank, the castle is protected on the landward side by a man-made moat hewn from the rock. The fortress was begun in the 12th century to guard the strategic river crossing into Wales, and was later extended in the 13th and 14th centuries. It was successfully beseiged in 1326 and subsequently destroyed by Parliamentary troops during the Civil War.

Goodrich Castle

The River Wye at Ross-on-Wye

The Market Hall, Ross-on-Wye

High on a sandstone cliff overlooking a large loop in the River Wye is the historic market town of **Ross-on-Wye**. Known as the "Gateway to the Wye Valley" it is justly a popular centre for exploring this outstandingly beautiful area. In the centre of the town stands the fine old Market Hall surrounded by attractive Georgian and Tudor buildings. One of these bears a plaque acknowledging it as the home of John Kyrle, a local philanthropist who died here in 1725. Known as "the Man of Ross" he lived in the town for most of his life and was responsible for laying out public gardens, repairing the church spire and giving Ross its first public water supply.

Ross-on-Wye from the River

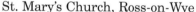

St. Mary's Church, Ross-on-Wye

St. Mary's Church in Ross was founded in the reign of King Stephen although most of the present structure dates from the 14th century. The spire is 208 feet high, a notable local landmark which is especially attractive reflected in the waters of the River Wye.

The **Plague Cross** which stands in the churchyard of the parish church recalls the terrible plague of 1637. In the space of two years it is recorded that five times as many people died in the area as were born here.

Ross-on-Wye from the river

Old Wye Bridge and Cathedral, Hereford

The River Wye flows through the city of **Hereford** and is spanned here by a six-arched stone bridge dating from the 15th century. Hereford has been the centre of a bishopric since AD 676 and the glory of the city is its 11th century pink sandstone cathedral which occupies a picturesque setting on the banks of the river. The fine Norman nave and the Lady Chapel are particularly delightful. The west front was originally built in the 14th century but much restoration work was carried out after a disastrous collapse in 1786 and also later in 1904. Within the cathedral are some unique possessions including the Mappa Mundi which dates from 1289 and is the largest known complete example of a map showing the world as it was believed to look at that time. The fine medieval chained library contains nearly 1500 books.

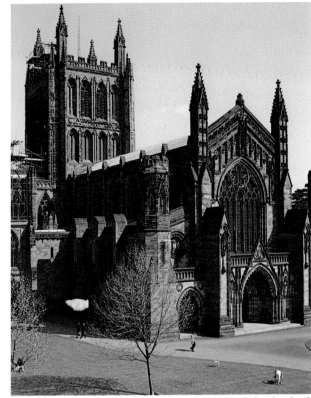

Hereford Cathedral

The Nave, Hereford Cathedral

At the heart of Hereford is High Town, the Saxon market centre of the city. As well as its market hall and shops, High Town contains many attractive 17th and 18th century buildings. The picturesque **Old House,** which dates from 1621, is the sole survivor of a row of houses known as Butcher's Row and was originally the Hall of the Guild of Butchers. This outstanding example of Jacobean domestic architecture is furnished in contemporary style and now houses a museum.

The Old House, Hereford

Broad Sreet, Hereford

From High Town there is access to the aptly named **Broad Street**. Leading from the ancient All Saints' Church at the northern end to the Cathedral at the southern, Broad Street also contains The City Museum and Art Gallery which features displays about the natural history, archaeology and history of Hereford and the surrounding area.

Behind the cathedral lie pleasan **Radcliffe Gardens**. Providing ; peaceful oasis in the centre of th town, the gardens slope away from the cathedral and meet the rive where it runs between Wye Bridg and Castle Green.

Herefordshire has changed very little over the centuries. Quiet country lanes, picturesque villages and ancient cottages still slumber in tranquil countryside which is rich in both scenery and history. Church Cottage at **Stretton Grandison**, a charming village which lies north east of Hereford, is typical of the splendid timber-framed buildings found in the area. Although altered and improved over centuries from their humble origins these delightful buildings are the epitome of old rural England.

Cottages at Stretton Grandison

Grange Court, Leominster

The fine old Herefordshire wool town of **Leominster** has a great variety of impressive architecture including the fine half-timbered Grange Court which dates from 1633 and the 11th century Priory which, according to tradition, was founded by Earl Leofric, the husband of Lady Godiva.

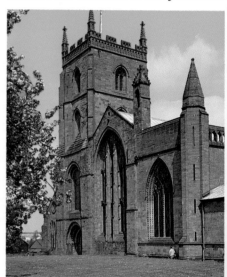

The Priory Church, Leominster

Leominster is the starting point of the **Black and White Village Trail**. About 40 miles in length, this circular route takes in many of the unspoiled black and white villages of north west Herefordshire. Among these are **Weobley**, with its abundance of timber-framed houses and inns which radiate out from the wide main street, and **Pembridge**. Here half-timbered cottages are grouped around the market place with its 14th century New Inn and Market Hall. Also noteworthy is Pembridge Church which has an unusual detached belfry. Returning towards Leominster the trail reaches **Eardisland**, perhaps the prettiest village in Herefordshire, which is famous for its wealth of timber and plaster buildings.

Cottage at Eardisland

Cottages at Pembridge

Red Lion Inn and Church, Weobley

Standing on the western slopes of the Malvern Hills near Ledbury is the beautiful old village of **Eastnor**. A church and a number of delightful timber-framed cottages with colourful gardens are grouped around the village green. Nearby Eastnor Castle, built in the Norman baronial style in 1812, stands in extensive parkland overlooking a lake. With turrets at each corner surrounding a central keep, the castle contains art treasures, furniture and a fine collection of armour.

The Old House, Bromyard

A market town rich in old houses, **Bromyard** has been a local centre since before the Domesday survey. Among its many fine buildings are the 16th century Bridge House, with some superb herringbone timber framing and a jettied front overhanging the street, and the half-timbered Falcon Hotel, an old coaching inn. Two miles eastwards is **Lower Brockhampton**, a splendid example of a half-timbered, moated manor house. It dates mainly from the 14th century and has an exceptionally well-preserved gatehouse over the moat. Built for a squire's son, this substantial homestead has a picturesque buckled roof of fine old tiles and a galleried dining-hall.

Lower Brockhampton

The Feathers Hotel, Ledbury

Equidistant from Hereford, Worcester and Gloucester, the attractive market town of **Ledbury** is surrounded by meadowland and streams, an excellent centre for exploring the Malvern Hills. Beloved by many poets including Wordsworth and the Brownings, Ledbury was the birthplace in 1878 of John Masefield who claimed that the area had profoundly influenced his poetry. A notable example of the town's Elizabethan architecture is the superb 16th century Feathers Hotel while, curving between fine half timbered cottages, little Church Lane leads up to the church with its elegant 202 feet high spire.

The historic **Market House** which stands in the square in Ledbury's main street is one of the most outstanding black-and white buildings in the area. It was built in 1633 by John Abel who was dubbed "King's Carpenter" by Charles I and is buried near the village of Weobley.

Ledbury from the Market House

The House on the Props is one of the oldest and most picturesque buildings in the town. Like the old Market House it is supported on wooden pillars with stone bases and its upper storey projects over the street.